I0122217

ILLEGAL IMMIGRATION AND THE DESTRUCTION OF AMERICA

Major (Ret.) James F. Linzey

LINZEY PUBLISHING HOUSE

ILLEGAL IMMIGRATION AND THE
DESTRUCTION OF AMERICA
Major (Ret.) James F. Linzey

Copyright © 2015 by James F. Linzey
All rights reserved under
International Copyright Conventions

Cover Design by Istvan Szabo, Ifj.
http://www.sapphireguardian.com

Printed in the United States of America
ISBN 978-1-936857-17-3

All rights reserved solely by the author. The author
guarantees all contents are original and do not infringe
upon the legal rights of any other person or work. No part
of this book may be reproduced in any form without the
permission of the author. The views expressed in this
book are not necessarily those of the publisher.

Linzey Publishing House
P.O. Box 300366
Escondido, California

OTHER BOOKS BY JAMES F. LINZEY

A Divine Appointment in Washington, DC
Baptism in the Spirit
The Holy Spirit
Moral Leadership
Why the Conservative Mind Matters
(Contributing author)

PREFACE

In November 1985, I was given a direct commission into the United States Air Force Reserves as a chaplain with the rank of first lieutenant. At the same time I was a schoolteacher in the Los Angeles Unified School District. I was in Watts not far from the horrifying beating of Reginald Denny, which was the beginning of severe rioting and looting. I was, in fact, driving out of Watts as that occurred, as quickly as I was allowed to drive by law, on my way to an event I had planned at Norton AFB in San Bernardino, California.

For several years up to that time, I had a surreal feeling that what I saw in society was not as it seemed to be. I could not pinpoint what I sensed, but it seemed like there was a subversive spirit undermining American society. Yet I could not substantiate it. No one told me this. I did not know what to do with what I sensed. So I began asking questions in the military to individuals only if I learned that they knew something I did not know, and if I felt safe to ask. Much to my amazement, I began learning things I did not know, which substantiated my discernment that something was dreadfully wrong in America.

The Dream

In January of 1987, I dreamed that I was in a concentration camp for Christians. I was in an area fenced in with a chain link fence that had barbed wire on top. The area seemed rectangular, front to back. Other Christians were in there with me. I don't know how many were there, but I remember seeing about a dozen or more people. We could not see the sky. For some reason it was not visible inside the compound. Perhaps the lack of a sky symbolized darkness. In front were some American soldiers. Suddenly they began mowing us down with automatic weapons. I found myself grabbing for metal folding chairs I had not previously seen, and, with others, I began shielding myself from the bullets. After a while it stopped.

From out of nowhere, Christians rushed to the front left corner of the compound in a panic and tried to climb over the fence. They failed to get over. Then they rushed to the front right corner and succeeded at getting over to escape the hellish nightmare. I joined them as fast as I could. As soon as I climbed over into freedom, I could see the clear blue sky.

Just then, as quick as we were free, I saw in the sky that they were coming for us. Helicopters were flying our way. We looked for a place to hide, but there was no place to go. The only object near us was a set of bleachers. And that was no place to hide, though some tried. We were again about to be arrested. Suddenly I woke up, startled.

Since then, I've had three more dreams similar to this one. The two following dreams were also in 1987. The fourth dream was in 2010.

The Role of America

Historically, the role of any nation's Armed Forces has been to secure its nation's borders, shores and airspace. But the United States is failing on all three fronts.

Historically, the role of any nation's government has been to establish and adhere to sound monetary policies. But the United States is spending itself purposely into oblivion, and it is being "told" what its policies will be and that she must adhere to them.

And, historically, the role of peace-loving nations has been to respect the sovereignty of all other nations and to attend to their own internal affairs. But the United States is too involved in the affairs of other nations, and it has allowed other nations to become too involved in the inner workings of the United States.

The contents of this book was originally prepared as a speech, prepared by my former college English professor who assisted me in the research and the writing. I am not an expert in the subject matter, but I sensed a "Call to Duty" to come to my country's aid to do my part to save her as any respectable human being would do, and as every minister of the Gospel is called to do, and to prevent what I saw in dreams from becoming a reality.

DEDICATION

*To The United States Armed Forces which has the
Constitutional duty to secure its nations' borders, shores,
and air space*

CONTENTS

INTRODUCTION

First let's be sure we understand the law.

Under Title 8, Section 1325 of the U.S. Code, "Improper Entry by Alien," means any citizen of any country other than the United States who

- Enters or attempts to enter the United States at any time or place other than as designated by immigration officers, or
- Eludes examination or inspection by immigration officers, or
- Attempts to enter or obtains entry to the United States by a willfully false or misleading representation or the willful concealment of a material fact, has committed a federal crime.

Violations of this law are punishable by criminal fines and imprisonment up to six months.

Immigration and Nationality Act Section 237 (a)(1)(B) says "any alien who is present in the United States in violation of this Act or any other law of the United States is deportable."

CHAPTER 1:
ILLEGAL IMMIGRATION –
A PROBLEM

Statistics

The Immigration and Naturalization Service (INS) estimates that in January of 2000 there were 7 million illegal aliens living in the United States. This number is growing by half a million a year. Thus, the illegal population in 2003 stood at least at 8 ½ million. Included in this estimate are approximately 78,000 illegal aliens from countries of special concern in the war on terror. The 500,000 annual increase in illegal aliens is the net growth in the illegal-alien population (new illegal immigration minus deaths, legalizations and out-migration) (Camarota, "Illegal Immigration," August 2004, 1).

The Census Bureau has estimates of its own. Its estimate at the 2000 Census suggests that the illegal population was about 8 million. If we use this number, we can conclude that the illegal alien population grew by half a million a year through the 1990s. This conclusion is verified by a draft report given to the House immigration subcommittee by the INS, estimating that the illegal population was 3.5 million in 1990. For the illegal population to have reached 8 million by 2000, the net increase had to be 400,000 to 500,000 per year during the 1990s (Camarota, 1).

The INS estimates that it gave out 1.5 million green cards to illegal aliens in the 1990s. This was not due to amnesty legislation, but it reflects how the legal immigration process embraces illegal immigration and encourages it through legal exemptions. According to the INS, only 412,000 illegal aliens were removed during the same decade (1990s), a pitiful 40,000 per year.

The impact on our society from such an influx of immigrants is astounding. In Los Angeles, 95 percent of all outstanding warrants for homicide (a total of 1,200–1,500) target illegal aliens. Up to two-thirds of all fugitive felony warrants (17,000) are for illegal aliens (MacDonald, 2).

A confidential California Department of Justice study reported in 1995 that 60 percent of the bloody 18th Street Gang in California is illegal (estimated membership: 20,000). Police officers say the proportion is undoubtedly much greater. The gang collaborates with the Mexican Mafia, the dominant force in California prisons, on complicated drug distribution schemes, extortion and drive-by assassinations. It is responsible for an assault or robbery every day in Los Angeles County. The gang has dramatically expanded over the last two decades by recruiting recently arrived youngsters from Central America and Mexico (MacDonald, 2, 3).

The leadership of the Columbia Li'l Cycos gang, which uses murder and racketeering to control the drug market around L.A.'s MacArthur Park, was about 60 percent illegal in 2002, says former Assistant U.S. Attorney Luis Li.

The LAPD and the Los Angeles City Attorney recently requested a judicial injunction against drug trafficking in Hollywood. The injunction targets the 18th Street Gang... and its non-gang members who sell drugs on behalf of the gang. Those "non-gang members" are virtually all illegal Mexicans, smuggled into the country by a trafficking ring organized by the 18th Street bigs (MacDonald, 3).

Mass Immigration

Free Republic reports these facts: Census 2000 results indicate that there were between 8 and 11 million illegal aliens living in the United States in 2000. The Center for Immigration Studies has reported that Census Bureau stats show that 700,000 to 800,000 new illegal aliens were settling in the U.S. each year during the late 1990s and that about 1 million settled in the most recent year of record. Far more enter each year, but there is a lot of back and forth. The 1 million represents illegals, who settle in for at least a couple of years.

According to *Free Republic,* a Conservative News Forum, mass illegal immigration is NOT inevitable. No nation can totally stop illegal immigration, but mass illegal immigration is preventable. The U.S. has mass illegal immigration because Congresses and Presidents have decided they want it, or at least that they will let it happen. In one action after another over the last decade, Congress has declined to approve measures known to effectively slow the illegal flow. Congress has also decided to end various kinds of enforcement that had been effective.

The 8 to 11 million illegal aliens that were residing in the U.S. in 2000 are a sign that the U.S. is losing control of its borders and losing the ability to determine who is a member of this national community. A country that has lost that ability also loses its ability to determine the rules of its society—to determine environmental protections, labor protections, health protections, and security/safety protections (*Free Republic,* 1). Today, unofficial estimates are that there are actually 30 million illegal aliens residing in the U.S. And If Barack Obama approves of amnesty, then this number would swell quickly to 100 million additional third worlders coming across our borders because the illegal aliens would then, legally, invite their relatives south of the border to come to the U.S. to live with them.

There is now a serious debate in Congress about whether the U.S. should even try to enforce its immigration laws. The debate is between "national-community Americans" (who believe in a separate, self-governed nation) and those who have a "post-American" vision (that America's workers be allowed to compete directly with every worker in the world and that global forces determine our quality of life rather than democratic self-determination).

The job of the INS is to ensure that those who should not be here will be required to leave. But Roy Beck, executive director of NumbersUSA.com, testified that the INS is "making virtually no effort to ensure that those who should not be here are required to leave" (*Free Republic*, 2). Our efforts on the border to keep illegal aliens out are failing. Beck reports that the word is out around the world: "If you can succeed in evading the U.S. Border Patrol on your way in, and if you do not commit an aggravated felony in the country, you have virtually no chance of ever being forced to leave." With an incentive like that, no wonder our borders are crowded (*Free Republic*, 2).

Who Cares?

Not politicians—they want more votes,
Not Big Business—it wants cheap labor,
Not union bosses—they want more members, more
    dues, more clout,
Not universities—they want more students, more
    grants, more diversity,
Not most voters—they want prosperity and fat
pocketbooks and are willing to "let Uncle Sam do it."

20

CHAPTER 2:
REASONS IMMIGRATION
IS A PROBLEM

Political Reasons

It is important to consider not only the economic, fiscal, cultural, and demographic impacts of immigration, but also the political impact.

The United States is currently experiencing the largest wave of immigration in its history (Poston, et.al, 1). By the end of the 1990s, over 1.5 million immigrants were arriving each year (legal and illegal). What most people do not realize is the way in which immigration impacts the distribution of seats in the United States House of Representatives. Apportionment is based on the total population of each state—including illegal aliens and all non-citizens. Estimates prepared by the Immigration and Naturalization Service (INS) indicate that almost seven million illegal aliens were counted in the 2000 Census (Poston, et. al, 1).

Article 1, section 2 of the U.S. Constitution mandates that a census be taken every ten years for the purpose of apportioning seats in the House of Representatives. The resident population of a state is all persons counted in the census, including those legal immigrants and illegal aliens who either mail their census forms back or who were contacted in an interview. A person is considered a state resident if he or she meets the Census' definition of "usual

21

residence" (i.e., he/she "has no other permanent place to stay" or lives there "most of the time"). All these people, including illegal aliens, were used to calculate the apportionment of seats in the House. There are currently 435 seats in the House (unchanged since 1911 when Congress fixed the number).

The INS conducted research to estimate the size of the illegal alien population, and it indicated that 6.6 million illegal aliens were counted in the 2000 Census. Immigration redistributes seats because the foreign-born population is so large and so concentrated—two-thirds live in just six states.

Since illegal aliens are very concentrated, with half living in just three states, the redistribution of seats in the House is significant politically (Poston, et. al., 3). If they were spread evenly over the country, they would have almost no impact at all on the political processes of our country. But as long as the number of immigrants entering remains at record levels and concentrates in a few states, immigration will continue to redistribute political power in Washington. Lower levels of immigration would mean a much smaller impact on the distribution of the House seats.

Though most of us believe that low-immigration states would be unaffected by such high counts of illegal aliens in our population, such states are in fact losing their political influence in Washington. Since the number of seats in the House of Representatives is definitive, if one state gains a seat because of an increase in population, another state must lose that same seat.

The INS report found that the presence of illegal aliens in other states caused Indiana, Michigan and Mississippi to each lose one seat in the House in 2000. Additionally, Montana failed to gain a seat it otherwise would have gained. None of those states lost a seat because of a decline in population; in fact the four states

22

had an increase in population of 1.6 million during the '90s (between the Census of 1990 and 2000). Three of those seats went to California, where one in seven residents is a non-citizen. Contrast the fact that one in fifty residents is a non-citizen in those states that lost seats; whereas one in ten residents is a non-citizen in New York, Texas, and Florida. These are the states that, along with California, have the highest number of illegal immigrants.

The same report explained that such redistribution of seats in the House would affect presidential elections because the Electoral College is based on the number of congressional delegates (Poston, et. al., 1).

Can illegal aliens be excluded? Excluding only illegal aliens from apportionment is a problem. It would be a politically popular idea, and it would seem to be fair, but it would be more difficult than excluding all non-citizens. The INS, the Census Bureau and other researchers estimate the number of illegal aliens, but they do not definitively identify individual illegal aliens in the Census. It is possible to simply ask respondents if they are illegal, but it seems certain that most would not identify themselves as illegal. Trying to exclude illegal aliens only is impractical, probably impossible.

Given the concentration of large numbers of illegal immigrants in the country, it is inevitable that they will exact a political cost. Because family relationships and existing cultural ties determine where immigrants live, trying to move them into new areas of the country will take many decades, if it is even possible. Thus, immigrants will continue to be concentrated in only a few states, and this concentration in turn will continue to shift political power in the House of Representatives and in the Electoral College (Poston, et. al., 8).

Domestic Reasons

Two main attractions for illegal aliens are jobs and family connections. The typical Mexican worker earns one-tenth what his American counterpart earns. Many American businesses are willing to hire cheap, compliant labor with no questions asked. Such businesses are seldom punished because our government lacks a viable system to verify new hires' work eligibility (Camarota, "High Cost," 1). Communities of recently arrived legal immigrants help create immigration networks used by illegal aliens and that serve as incubators for illegal immigration. They provide jobs, housing and a means of entering the United States (Camarota, "High Cost," 1).

G. Russell Evans, a Captain in the U.S. Coast Guard (Ret) and a columnist and author, writes in his article "Blame Greed for Runaway Immigration," June 3, 2002, that one of the greatest threats to America is the runaway flood of immigrants, both legal and illegal. He believes it can conceivably make America a Third World-style country. Who is to blame? Evans blames greedy politicians in Washington who are after potential immigrant votes.

Failure to enforce immigration laws leads to much broader problems. For one, there is the nearly total loss of control over immigration policy. Fifty years ago, immigration policy may have driven immigration numbers, but today the numbers drive the policy. The non-stop increase of legal and illegal aliens is reshaping the language and the law to dissolve any distinction between legal and illegal immigration, and ultimately, any distinction between national borders (MacDonald, 1).

National Security

Three of the 9/11 hijackers were illegal visa overstayers. Seven of the nineteen obtained fraudulent ID cards with the help of illegal alien day laborers in

24

Virginia. Two of the 1993 World Trade Center bombers were illegal aliens. At least one al Qaeda-linked operative, convicted in the World Trade Center bombing plot, obtained amnesty through a program intended for farmworkers. Who knows how many more are lurking among us as amnestied American citizens? More than 115,000 people from Middle Eastern countries are here illegally. More than 1,000 of them were smuggled through Mexico by convicted global crime ringleader George Tajirian. Some 6,000 Middle Eastern men who have defied deportation orders remain on the loose, reports Michelle Malkin, in her article "*The Wall Street Journal* on Illegal Immigration: Bordering on Idiocy" (April 25, 2002, Internet).

According to Art Moore's article, "Illegal Immigration Fueling aims of Hispanic Radicals" (2002) (World Net Daily.com), the radical Hispanic movement has a dream of retaking the southwestern United States. Mexican and U.S. policies are helping rather than hindering that dream. Glenn Spencer, president of Voices of Citizens Together, agrees that there is an idea of a radical takeover when he says, "A massive influx of illegal immigrants is 'importing poverty' and growing an ethnic community with greater loyalty to Mexico than the U.S." (Moore, 1). Spencer told World Net Daily, "Unless this is shut down..., I believe that it will be irreversible, and that it will most certainly lead to a breakup of the United States" (Moore, 1).

A breakaway of the U.S. states is a distinct possibility, according to prominent Chicano activist and University of California at Riverside professor Armando Navarro. In an interview with World Net Daily, Navarro said "that if demographic and social trends continue, secession is inevitable" (Moore, 1).

Navarro notes that most studies show that within the next twenty to thirty years Latinos will comprise more than 50 percent of the population of California. This majority will open the door for "the idea of an Aztlan." Chicano folklore regards Aztlan, the mythical birthplace of the Aztecs, as an area that includes California, Arizona, Nevada, New Mexico and parts of Colorado and Texas. Spencer believes the aim is to create a sovereign state, the "Republica del Norte," that would combine the American Southwest with the Northern Mexican states and eventually merge with Mexico. "I see that as a goal of many Mexicans," Spencer said (Moore, 1).

In a 1997 speech in Chicago to the "National Council of La Raza," a Hispanic advocacy group, former Mexican President Ernesto Zedillo said that he "proudly affirmed that the Mexican nation extends beyond the territory enclosed by its borders and that Mexican migrants are an important part of this" (Moore, 2). Because of this belief, the Mexican government proposed a constitutional amendment that allows Mexican citizens to hold dual citizenship. Spencer believes the object of this vote is to enable Mexicans in the United States to vote in the interests of Mexico (Moore, 2).

Misguided U.S. policies and lax enforcement of the immigration laws have allowed a steady stream of 1 million illegal immigrants a year to enter the country. Demographers agree that instead of integrating into a "melting pot," new Hispanic immigrants, both legal and illegal, are building a distinct, politically active community (Moore, 3).

Other concerns about National Security have to do with border control. Though the U.S. has tripled its border patrol budget over the past five years, the flow of immigrants has barely changed. Mexican President Vicente Fox has pushed for an eventual erasure of the southern border and encouraged Mexicans to seek work in the U.S. At a speech in 2001, at a border post in Nogales just south of the Arizona border, Fox said, "We want to salute these heroes, these kids leaving their homes,... with tears in their eyes,... to set out on a difficult... search for a job, an opportunity they can't find at home" (Moore, 3). Under the Fox regime, Mexico has an Office for Mexicans Abroad that provides survival kits for Mexicans who seek to enter the U.S. illegally (Moore, 3).

But Allan Wall, an American married to a Mexican and a resident south of the border for ten years, says that immigration is not helping Mexico. Wall, a Mexican correspondent for *Project U.S.A.*, an immigration reform group in New York, said, "It's kind of like welfare; it encourages people to use the U.S. as a safety net rather than solve the problems in Mexico" (Moore, 3). Wall agrees that the influx is precipitating a demographic meltdown that could lead to a fracturing of the country. He said, "The U.S. needs to drastically reduce immigration and go back to an assimilation model, where immigrants learn English and become American; otherwise it will be a disaster" (Moore, 4).

Terrorism

Some of the most violent criminals at large today are illegal aliens. In cities where crime is highest, though, the police cannot use the most obvious tool to apprehend them—they cannot deport them as illegal aliens. In Los Angeles, for example, dozens of gang members from a Salvadoran prison gang have sneaked back into town after having been deported for such crimes as murder, shootings and drug trafficking. Police officers know who the criminals are and know that their being in this country is a felony. But the LAPD has a rule against enforcing immigration law. This ban on immigration enforcement is the same in many immigrant-heavy cities across the country—in New York, Chicago, Austin, San Diego and Houston for example. These policies—called "sanctuary policies"—prohibit a city's employees, including the police, from reporting immigration violations to federal authorities (MacDonald, 1).

Sanctuary laws show the political power of immigrant lobbies. The demographic clout is so powerful that the LAPD police captain said, "We can't even talk about it... People are afraid of a backlash from Hispanics" (MacDonald, 1).

In September 2003, MacDonald asked the Miami Police Department's spokesman, Detective Delrish Moss, about his employer's policy about illegal lawbreakers. His response: "We have shied away from unnecessary involvement dealing with immigration issues," explained Detective Moss, choosing his words carefully, "because of our large immigration population" (MacDonald, 2).

When police officers cannot discuss the problem of illegals because it will seem like a gross social faux pas, something not to be done in polite company, it is time to change. At the same time that this ban is imposed on police officers, the millions of illegal aliens go on working, shopping, traveling and committing crimes in plain view, utterly confident in their de facto immunity from the immigration law (Mac Donald, 2).

The visa lottery is possibly the strangest contributor to terrorism. Our government actually runs a system where people send in postcards, and then names are drawn out of a hat, with 50,000 winners each year receiving permanent residence in the United States. This now takes place electronically. The winners need not have even one family member in the United States, or any job skill that is supposed to be needed, nor any compelling humanitarian reason for being in the U.S. All they need is the desire to come to the United States. There are many problems with the visa lottery, but probably the most significant is that it creates a great opportunity for terrorists (Camarota, "Visa," 1).

Any fraud is bad, but after the September 11 attacks, immigration fraud of any kind poses a dire security risk and threat. The lottery does not draw people randomly from around the globe. Winners come disproportionately from countries that were part of the special registration system for temporary visitors set up after 9/11. About one-third of the winners comes from those countries of special concern in the war against Islamic extremism.

Several lottery winners have already been involved in terrorism in the United States. Karim Koubriti, convicted in 2002 on terrorism-related charges, was a lottery winner from Morocco, as was Ahmed Hannan, who was acquitted of terrorism charges in the same trial but convicted of document fraud. The most notorious lottery winner is Hesham Mohamed Hedayet (Camarota, "Visa," 2).

The lottery is ideal for terrorists because it encourages immigration from those parts of the world where fraud is common, documents are difficult to verify and al-Qaeda is very active. It also allows people into the country with no family or other significant connections to the United States. This is tailor-made for someone wishing to attack our country. A green card is far more valuable to terrorists than a temporary visa. A green card lets a person stay in the country indefinitely, which gives terrorists the time they may need to plan a sophisticated plot. Moreover, permanent residency allows the recipients to work at almost any jobs they like, get licenses to handle hazardous material and travel to and from the United States as often as they please. If one were to design a visa that was ideal for terrorists, the visa lottery system would be it (Camarota, 3).

Failures in our immigration system result mostly from lack of resources and ill-conceived immigration programs. The visa lottery is clearly one of those ill-conceived programs. The lottery does not increase diversity, serve any economic need, promote humanitarian goals or help families reunite. It creates a huge burden for the immigration system, encourages illegal immigration, invites fraud and makes it easier for terrorists to enter.

The politics of terrorism and immigration have had deleterious effects in New York. Former New York Mayor Rudolph Giuliani sued all the way to the Supreme Court to defend the city's sanctuary policy against Congressional override. He sued to declare the 1996 federal ban on sanctuary policies unconstitutional, and, though he lost in court, he remained defiant. On September 5, 2001, his handpicked charter revision committee ruled that New York may still require that its employees keep immigration information confidential to preserve trust between immigrants and government. Six days later, several former visa-overstayers conducted the most devastating attack in history—on the city of New York and the country (MacDonald, 4).

If a Mexican day laborer can sneak across the border, so can an al-Qaeda terrorist. While the vast majority of illegals are not terrorists, the fact that hundreds of thousands of people are able to settle in the United States illegally each year shows that terrorists who wish to do so face few obstacles. We cannot protect ourselves from terrorism without dealing with illegal immigration (Krikorian, "Securing," 8).

CHAPTER 3:
BORDERS ARE CRUCIAL

Borders have both instrumental and symbolic functions. The instrumental functions simply mark the line on the ground where one country ends and another begins. But the symbolic significance may be even more important in some cases. Symbolically, borders are about image and resources and reputation. Power depends not only on physical abilities and coercion, says Peter Andreas, but also on legitimacy and symbolic representation (143). Anthony C. Cohen adds that a border "encapsulates the identity of a community" through the interaction of its members with other communities" (12). Consequently a border's line on the ground may not be as significant as its line in the collective minds of citizens.

Many people believe that borders will eventually melt away, resulting in what business consultant Kenichi Ohmae calls a "borderless world" (Custred, 1). It is true that some borders are eroding, but others are undergoing transformations of a different kind. Although some believe that borders no longer really matter, borders do indeed matter and will continue to matter for some time to come. As an example, let's look at the borders of North America.

Canada
The United States-Canada border, extending from the Pacific to the Atlantic, stretches some 4,000 miles across

the countries. If we add Alaska, British Columbia and the Yukon Territory, the border between the United States and Canada is some 8,000 miles long (Gibbons, 316). It is designated the longest undefended border in the world. Such a fact reflects the similarities between the two countries—that it is not necessary to defend the long border. The fact is also important given the physical proximity of the majority of the Canadian people to the border. Four-fifths of the population of Canada lives only about 150 kilometers from the border (Gibbons, 317). Consequently, one of the differences between the two countries is that Canada is a borderland society in contrast to the United States where the northern border plays almost no role at all in the national consciousness.

The Friendship Arch on the U.S.-Canada border in Blaine, Washington, proclaims the two countries as "Children of a Common Mother." The inscription asserts both the cultural unity and the political separateness of the two countries. Some 200 million people cross the border every year (Custred, 1), and the economic trade between the two may be the largest in the world. Though there are probably no two countries in the world more alike than the United States and Canada (demographically, socially, economically, linguistically and culturally), there are still many differences that distinguish them.

One major difference is national identity. Because Canada has two founding nations, the country has struggled with its own identity. Another difference is Canada's willingness to accept twice as many immigrants and four times as many asylum seekers each year (as a proportion of its population) as the United States is willing to receive. Visas are not always necessary for entry into Canada (because of her liberal asylum policy) (Bisset, 12). Newcomers can simply get on an airplane and request asylum on arrival—with no documents at all.

Asylum seekers are given insurance, driver's licenses and subsidies until their cases are heard. In the meantime, they are free to roam the country and to cross the border into the United States if they wish.

Such freedom granted to Canadian immigrants may pose hazards for the United States. After September 11, David Harris said that at least fifty known terrorist groups were inside Canada, ranging from the IRA to Hezbollah, Hamas and al-Qaeda. "Canada," says Harris, "has everything for the discriminating terrorist.... Indeed, Canada is the 'weak link' in America's defense against terrorist operations" (quoted in Custred, 3). Custred feels that our danger may be in the fact that on our "northern flank is a neighbor that disregards document fraud, maintains lax visa practices, and has the most generous asylum policy in the world" (3).

Mexico

The United States-Mexico border extends about 2,000 miles from the Pacific Ocean to the Gulf of Mexico. This border is also heavily traveled, with over 274 million crossings in 2002 alone (U.S. Dept. of Homeland Security). The largest traffic corridor is the San Diego-Tijuana metropolitan area with a combined population of over 4.1 million people. The level of trust and cooperation between American and Mexican authorities is quite different from that of the U.S.-Canadian border. Mexican identity tends to be defined by opposition to the United States rather than cooperation, like Canada.

Some people return south to Mexico though most of the crossing is north to the U.S. Hundreds of Mexicans every year who have been found liable for damages in American civil courts or who are fugitives from the law in the United States find safe haven simply by slipping back across the border into Mexico (Custred, 3). Mexico is also a potential haven for those criminals most dangerous to society.

Consequently, we see that borders divide countries that have different levels of toleration for and different ways of dealing with safety issues and political problems. Agreements are often differently understood and differently respected.

The Mexican border also faces another problem however. It also is a divide between the prosperity of the developed world and the relative poverty of the Third World. In fact, the United States-Mexico border is the only land border in the world between those two important zones. The difference can be experienced directly when one crosses the border from Nogales, Sonora, to Nogales, Arizona. The differences are in the physical appearances and qualities of the two cities rather than in the culture of the people (96 percent of the people on the U.S. side of the line are of Mexican descent) (Custred, 4).

Mexico is also a means to an end. Illegal aliens from Central America cross Mexico's southern border with Guatemala to make a quick transit through Mexico to the United States (Grayson, 10). Illegal Mexican immigrants to the United States are often seen as "heroes" by the Mexican elite. Why? The exodus from Mexico of low-skilled labor acts as a safety valve for Mexican society as well as the source of a $10 billion flow of money in the form of remittances from Mexicans working in the United States (*The Arizona Republic*, 1/25/2003).

To take even more advantage of these rewards, Mexico has changed its designation from a Latin American country to a North American country. It has asked for EU-styled borders within NAFTA, and it has realigned its policies along the lines of an ethnic, rather than a territorial, nation-state. With this definition, a Mexican is a Mexican no matter where he lives (Aquilar Zinser, 2001 (a), 2001 (b)).

Though the United States gives little thought to the northern border, the Mexican border is generally considered a problem for the American people. There is a sharp division between the American and Mexican peoples, and there are many perceived stereotypes of criminal activities associated with the Mexican border towns. Illegally crossing the border has brought many personal, social, economic, political and domestic concerns.

Jon E. Dougherty documents in his book *Illegals: The Imminent Threat Posed by Our Unsecured U.S.-Mexico Border* that Mexico is simply not taking responsibility for its primary role in the U.S. illegal immigrant problem (1). Mexico, in fact, encourages its citizens to break into the United States (1). Anyone who has heard about Mexico has heard of its dirt, poverty, underfed children and unemployment. We believe that Mexico is poor. Dougherty points out that Mexico has a lot of poverty, but it is not poor. Mexico is rich in natural resources, and should it tap those resources, it has the capacity to obliterate much of that poverty (Dougherty, "Mexico," 1). Dougherty states "Mexico is the richest nation in Latin America when measured by GDP.... In 2001 Mexico's GDP was the highest in Latin America, a substantial 22.5 % more than runner-up Brazil" ("Mexico" 2.).

Why so much poverty then? Dougherty says it's simple: The country's elite won't allow the poor to have opportunities. Economist Gary Hufbauer of the Institute for International Economics writes, "Basically, the wealthy classes do not want to tax themselves, period" (Dougherty, "Mexico," 2). "The immigration scam is very successful: The rulers of Mexico export their unemployment to the United States and get back billions in remittance cash annually—2003 racked up a record $11 billion," writes Brenda Walker for VDARE.com

(Dougherty, "Mexico," 3).

Borders matter. The borders of North America are no different from other borders of the world. North American borders are unique, though, since they divide one of the earth's seven continents into three separate nation-states that differ significantly. Mexico may be the most advanced nation in Latin America, yet it still struggles to rise from Third World status. The United States is the pre-eminent economic, political, cultural and military power in the world. Canada is a highly developed country, and it would not at all be considered diminished as a country if it were not for its larger neighbor to the south. But since these differences remain, it is important to keep the borders separate and distinguishable.

CHAPTER 4:
COSTS OF IMMIGRATION

The impact on the average citizen of the United States is not easy to assess. Even though most Americans are aware that immigration, especially illegal immigration, is not really beneficial, it is hard to convince someone of how much it is costing in social costs, and how much it might be costing in lost wages.

The Americans for Immigration Control, based in Merrifield, VA, has released frightening, documented findings.

- U.S. services and benefits given to legal and illegal immigrants cost American taxpayers $68 billion per year—and that number is growing.
- Bilingual education doubles the cost of schooling aliens.
- English as our language is under assault—with driver's licenses, voting ballots and citizenship ceremonies offered in dozens of languages.
- 400,000 foreigners now collect Social Security benefits without ever working a single day in America. Immigrants get Medicaid twice as often as native citizens.
- Immigration costs U.S. born workers $133 billion per year in job losses.
- Over 25 percent of federal prisoners are immigrants.
- Illegal aliens commit 12 percent of felonies, 25 percent of burglaries and 34 percent of car thefts.

- Non-citizens collect $7 billion per year in welfare, including medical assistance, food stamps, housing—courtesy of taxpayers (and members of Congress who allow it to happen).
- Two-thirds of U.S. population growth is due to our immigration policy.

Border counties are often among the poorest in the country, and yet they are forced to bear the financial burdens of immigrant-induced costs. Those costs include costs to the criminal justice system as well as to the emergency medical system. Property owners suffer financial damage due to mass migration across their land—many live in fear in their own homes (Custred, 6). National parks near the border also suffer environmental damage because of the sheer numbers of people crossing the border through the parks.

Illegal immigration also contributes to the dramatic population growth overwhelming some communities across the United States—crowding school classrooms, consuming already limited affordable housing, and straining precious natural resources like water, energy and forestland. The illegal population puts an enormous drain on public funds. The small amount of taxes some of them do pay in no way covers the services received by them.

While illegal aliens are not supposed to use most welfare programs, they do in fact use them. Even if the immigrant himself is not eligible because of legal status, immigrant families can still receive benefits on behalf of their U.S. born children, whose welfare eligibility is the same as any other native-born American (Krikorian, "Securing," 3). The research of the Center for Immigration Studies indicated that 31 percent of the households headed by illegal aliens from Mexico use at least one major welfare program (Krikorian, "Securing," 3).

In 1997, the National Academy of Sciences (NAS) estimated that immigrant households consume between $11 billion and $20 billion more in public services than they pay in taxes each year. The NAS estimated that each immigrant with less than a high school education imposes a net fiscal drain of $89,000 on public coffers during his lifetime (Krikorian, "Security," 3).

CHAPTER 5:
SOLUTIONS

The overmatch between immigration authorities and the numbers of illegal immigrants seems to prohibit the deportation of the illegal aliens. Even where the ICE successfully nabs and deports criminal aliens, the reality is that they all come back. They can't make it in Mexico, so they just wait a while (a few hours or a few days), and they return. The tens of thousands of illegal farmworkers and restaurant dishwashers who overpower the U.S. border control every year carry hundreds or even thousands of criminals and assailants and terrorists with them. The criminal element uses the same smuggling industry as the "good" illegal aliens, and they benefit from the same odds—there are so many more of them than there are of the border patrol (Camarota, "Visa Lottery," 1).

Lack of resources hinders deportation too. In theory, a judge can order an illegal deported. But the ICE lacks manpower to do so. In theory, they can put the illegal on a bus and take him across the border, but they usually do not have the manpower to enforce the bus ride. Second alternative: Put the alien in detention pending deportation. But again, there is no space and no staff in proportion to the demand. The agency's actual response to final orders of removal is what is known as a "run letter." A run letter is a notice that immigration authorities send to a deportable alien requesting that he kindly show up in a month to be deported (at a time when the agency hopes to have officers to deport the alien). The results are obvious—in 2001, 87 percent of the deportable aliens who received "run letters" disappeared. The number was even higher—94 percent—if the alien was from a terror-sponsoring country (Camarota, "Visa," 3).

The elite who profit from the illegal work force believe that immigration is inevitable. That is not true. Immigration can take place only if there are networks of relatives, friends or other countrymen directing immigrants to a particular place. These networks come only because government policies of not enforcing the law permit networks to grow. Interrupting such networks is harder than creating them, but it is possible. After all, the trans-Atlantic immigration networks from the turn of the last century were successfully interrupted; in fact, they atrophied completely (Krikorian, *Nat'l Rev.*, 2).

To find an employer guilty of violating the ban on hiring illegal aliens, immigration authorities must prove that the employer knew he was being given fake papers—an almost impossible burden of proof. Meanwhile, the market for counterfeit documents has exploded. In one month alone in 1998, the INS seized nearly two million counterfeit documents in Los Angeles—all destined for workers, welfare seekers, criminals and terrorists (MacDonald, 4).

The only way to dampen illegal immigration is to remove the job magnet. As long as migrants believe they can easily get work, they will find ways to evade border controls. But the enforcement of laws against illegal labor is at the absolute bottom of the government's priorities (MacDonald, 5).

Myths and Lies

A few of the more common Myths and Lies are these:

1. **America has lots of room to double the population.**
   The open spaces one sees from an airplane are not
   the places the millions of new immigrants and their
   families will settle—they will go to the already
   overcrowded urban parts of our country.
2. **Americans won't do the work illegals do.** In the
   areas where no illegals live, the grass is still getting
   cut, meat is still being packed, houses are still being
   cleaned, the fruit is still being picked. Those in favor
   of illegal labor are businesses that are addicted to
   cheap labor. If Americans care about the country's
   future, they will realize that consumers who favor
   exploiting illegal workers because it keeps prices
   down are thinking of the short term only. In the long
   run, our country will suffer.
3. **Illegal aliens are better off in the U.S. doing menial
   jobs than they are in their own countries.** Perhaps in
   the short run. But American's exploitation of
   immigrants remains in the minds of their children
   for generations to come, creating resentment of
   America even in the assimilation of American-born
   offspring.
4. **The cost of not educating undocumented children is
   higher than the cost of educating them.**
   Undocumented children are citizens of another
   country that is responsible for their education.
   California schools have a "don't ask, don't tell"
   policy regarding who gets to go to school. This
   policy is a powerful magnet that attracts illegals to
   California. The costs are enormous—notice
   California's struggle for financial survival.
5. **Illegal alien farmworkers come to the U.S. for jobs
   that Americans won't take, so they should be given
   temporary visas to allow them to work the fields.**

Almost all of these workers sooner or later head for the cities for better jobs, and they bring their families in too

In an article titled "Remaking the Political Landscape: The Impact of Illegal and Legal Immigration on Congressional Apportionment," October 2003, Dudley L. Poston, Jr., Steven A. Camarota and Amanda K. Baumle wrote that one way to address the problem would be for the U.S. to encourage legal immigrants to naturalize. This would not correct the problem of illegal aliens though, nor would it change the fact that low-immigration states are losing political power. As long as one million or more immigrants are allowed in each year, the non-citizen population will continue to grow even though the number of naturalizations increases as well. In the 1990s, the number of naturalizations increased, but the number of non-citizens increased dramatically to 18.5 million in 2000 from 11.8 million in 1990 (and 7 million in 1980) (2, 1).

Other solutions are untenable. The expansion of border enforcement is ineffectual. The Border Patrol has doubled since 1996—its 10,000 agents are better equipped and doing a better job than ever before. But the Border Patrol alone cannot control illegal immigration.

Enforce Immigrations Laws

The standard response to illegal immigration has been increased border enforcement. The border does indeed need to be tightened. But the border is not enough. No attention has been paid to law enforcement at work sites within the United States. Nor has any attention been paid to networks created by high levels of legal immigration— and to how they contribute to mass illegal immigration.

Most people think we have a choice of only two responses to illegal aliens living in the U.S.—either launch mass roundups and deport over nine million people, or legalize their staying in the U.S.

In fact, most of Congress laughs at the idea of enforcing the law to deport illegal aliens. One commentator in *The Wall Street Journal* stated that enforcing the law is not possible, that it is a "fantasy" of the "extreme, restrictionist" right wing. Manhattan Institute's Tamar Jacoby wrote in *The New Republic* of "futile law enforcement" and how "the migrant flow is inevitable" (Mark Krikorian. "Not Amnesty but Attrition: The Way to go on Immigration," *National Review*, March 22, 2004, 1).

Amnesty

Amnesty is the option with the largest controversy—it is the choice of many congressional proposals. The 245(I) provision of federal immigration law will allow "illegal aliens who have found employer or family sponsors to obtain visas in the U.S. for a $1,000 fee" instead of being forced to return home. The provision also allows these applicants to bypass a 1996 federal law barring illegal aliens from re-entering the U.S. for up to ten years. The amnesty would be extended to any law-breaking alien from any country that can hustle up an American employer or a "spouse" and pay a good immigration lawyer. Amnesty is an open invitation for marriage fraud, document fraud and endless litigation. It is a known loophole for terrorists.

Advocates for amnesty argue that it is the only solution to the illegal alien crisis because law enforcement clearly won't work. Actually, though, many believe that law enforcement has not really been tried. No effort has been expended to make the laws work. However, amnesty has been tried—in the industrial strength version of 1986 and the more limited doses ever since. Clearly amnesty has been a failure (MacDonald, 3). Before we try amnesty again, and fail again, perhaps it's time to try something else.

The INS report clearly demonstrates that amnesties do not solve the problem of illegal immigration. Table C, p. 10, of the Report shows that those who received amnesty in 1986 were entirely replaced by new illegal aliens, so that the number of illegal aliens was higher than ever in just a few years. Mark Krikorian points out that amnesty does not solve the problem of future illegal immigration. After the last amnesty in 1986, the 2.7 million illegal aliens who were given green cards were entirely replaced by new illegal aliens within less than ten years (Krikorian, "Securing," 6).

In the past, amnesties have helped terrorists, not impeded them in any way. Mahmud "The Red" Abouhalima, an Egyptian illegal alien working as a cab driver in New York, received amnesty under the 1986 Immigration and Reform and Control Act, falsely claiming to be an agricultural worker. Issuing Mahmud Abouhalima a green card facilitated his terrorism because he could then work at any job he wished and was able to travel to and from the United States freely. According to the October 4, 1993, issue of *Time* magazine, it was only after he received his green card in 1990 that he went to Pakistan to receive combat training. So it was the green card through amnesty that made his training by al-Qaeda and his terrorism possible.

Attrition

Krikorian offers a third option between the politically impossible mass roundups and the surrender of our sovereignty touted by the open-borders liberals. The third way is attrition—squeezing the illegal population through consistent, across-the-board law enforcement to bring about an annual reduction in the illegal population (rather than the annual increases we have seen for more than a decade) (Krikorian, *Nat'l Rev.*, 1).

According to a 2003 INS report, thousands of people stop being illegal aliens each year. From 1995–1999, 165,000 a year went home, the same number got legal status, 50,000 were deported, and 25,000 died. That is more than 400,000 each year subtracted from the resident illegal population. That's great. The problem, though, is that the average inflow of new illegal aliens was nearly 800,000—double the outflow—an average increase of 400,000.

The solution is to increase the number of people leaving each year, and to decrease the number of new illegal settlers each year, so that there is an annual decline in the total number of illegals.

This is not an immediate, magical solution (there is no magic), but over time it would help us out of a crisis situation (*Nat'l Rev.*, 1).

An attrition policy would have two key components:
- First, it would include more law enforcement— arrests, prosecutions, deportations and asset seizures.
- Second, it would require verification of legal status at a variety of important choke points to make it difficult and unpleasant to live here illegally.

When the U.S. increased immigration enforcement against Middle Easterners (and only Middle Easterners) after 9/11, Pakistanis, which were the largest group of illegals from that part of the world, fled the country in droves to avoid being caught in the dragnet (Krikorian, *Nat'l Rev.*, 2).

Another enforcement of deportation came inadvertently. The Social Security Administration, in 2002, sent out almost a million "no-match" letters to employers that filed W-2s with information inconsistent with SSA's records. The intention was to clear up misspellings, name changes and other mistakes. But most of the problem was caused by illegal aliens lying to their employers, and thousands of illegals quit or were fired when they were found out (Krikorian, *Nat'l Rev.*, 2).

When we actually enforce the law, illegal immigration is eroded. Enforcement measures will remove some illegals, but the majority of illegals will need to be persuaded to deport themselves. The "choke-points" will get many illegal aliens to leave because those points are set at events that are necessary for life. For example, people have to work, so requiring proof of legal status upon starting a job would serve as a choke point. Other possible points would include getting a driver's license, registering an automobile, opening a bank account, applying for a car loan or a mortgage, enrolling children in public schools, getting a business license and enrolling in medical insurance. Consistent enforcement of these proofs is all we need (Krikorian, *Nat' Rev.*, 3).

CHAPTER 6:
CONCLUSION

If one can say that anything came out of the atrocities of 9/11, perhaps it is that many Americans have now come to realize that immigration is not simply a matter of economics or something to think about in romantic or nostalgic terms. Quaint stories of one's immigrant grandmother can no longer be a substitute for intelligent discourse on one of the most important issues confronting this country today.

Most Americans want something done about immigration. However, most are afraid to speak out because they don't want to be labeled as racist, or as anti-immigrant. Most afraid are those who live near thousands of immigrants. Perhaps we should realize that this fear is one of the weapons used to stop any action against immigration. It's an effective weapon, and those who profit from illegal immigration use it freely.

Because it is a public policy issue, it needs to be debated. Unfortunately, the press tends to give only one side of the whole issue. To get the facts, then, it is necessary to search on our own. Wall believes we need to distinguish between 'anti-immigrant" and "anti-immigration," but this kind of separation is not always easy, though, unless we know immigrants personally.

To end illegal immigration requires the enforcement of stringent measures. Those measures would ensure that people who enter illegally or overstay their lawful status will not be able to obtain employment, public assistance benefits, public education, public housing or any other taxpayer-funded benefit without detection. Effective control and management of the laws against illegal immigration require adequate resources. But those costs will be more than offset by savings to states, counties, communities and school districts across the nation.

BIBLIOGRAPHY AND FURTHER READING

Andreas, Peter. 2000. *Border Games: Policing the U.S.-Mexico Divide*. Ithaca, N. Y.: Cornell University Press.

Aquilar Zinser, Adolfo. 2001. "La Noche de la Migra." *El Siglo ael Torreon*. May 5.

Bisset, James. "Canada's Asylum System: a Threat to American Security?" *Backgrounder*. Washington D. C.: Center for Immigration Studies. http://www.cis.org/articles/2002/back402.html.

Camarota, Steven A. 2004. "The High Cost of Cheap Labor: Illegal Immigration and the Federal Budget." Center Paper 23, August.

Camarota, Steven A. "Immigrants in the United States—2002: A Snapshot of America's Foreign-Born Population." www.cis.org/aritcles/2002/back1302.html.

Camarota, Steven. 2004. "What's Wrong with the Visa Lottery?" Testimony before the U.S. House of Representatives Committee on the Judiciary Subcommittee on Immigration, Border Security, and Claims. April 29.

Census Bureau. American Community Survey collected in 2002. http://www.census.gov/acs/www/Products/index.htm.

Census Bureau Report (containing estimates of illegal population by country of origin) can be found at: http://www.census.gov/population/www/documentat ion/twpsoo61.html. See Table A-6, p. 36.

Cohen, Anthony C. 1985. *The Symbolic Construction of Community.* New York: Tavistock Publications.

Custred, Glynn. 2003. "North American Borders: Why They Matter. Internet." April.

Dougherty, Jon. E. 2004. "Exporting Jobs, Importing Cheaper Wages." Newsmax.com. February.

Dougherty, Jon E. 2004. "Illegals: The Imminent Threat Posed by Our Unsecured U.S.-Mexico Border."

Dougherty, Jon. E. 2004. "Mexico Encourages Illegal Immigration." Newsmax.com. Feb. 27.

Evans, G. Russell, Capt. 2002. "Blame Greed for Runaway Immigration." Americanism Educational League of Buena Park, Calif. June 3.

INS report can be found at: http://uscis.gov/graphics/shared/aboutus/statistics/III Report 1211.pdf.

Gibbins, Roger. 1997. "The Meaning and Significance of the American-Canadian Border." In *Borders and Border Regions of Europe and North America,* eds. Paul

Ganster, et. al. San Diego: San Diego State University Press.

Grayson, George. "Mexico's Forgotten Southern Border." *Backgrounder.* Washington D. C.: Center for Immigration Studies. http://www.cis.org/araticles/2002/back702.html.

Krikorian, Mark. 2002. "Arizona Amnesty: Rewarding Illegal Aliens." *National Review Online.* November 21.

Krikorian, Mark. 2004. "Not Amnesty but Attrition: The Way to go on Immigration." *National Review,* March 22.

Krikorian, Mark. 2004. "Playing Games with Security: Taking Two Steps Back for every Step Forward on Immigration." Op-ed *National Review Online,* August 18.

Krikorian, Mark. 2004. "Post-Americans: They've just grown beyond their Country." Op-ed. *National Review Online,* June 22.

Krikorian, Mark. 2003. "Securing the Homeland Through Immigration Law Enforcement." Testimony prepared for the U.S. House of Representatives, Committee on the Judiciary. Subcommittee on Immigration, Border Security, and Claims, Department of Homeland Security Transition: Bureau of Immigration and Customs Enforcement. April 10.

MacDonald, Heather. 2004. "Crime and the Illegal Alien: The Fallout from Crippled Immigration Enforcement." *City Journal.* June.

MacDonald, Heather. 2004. "The Illegal-Alien Crime Wave." *City Journal.* Winter.

Malkin, Michelle. 2002. *"The Wall Street Journal* on Illegal Immigration: Bordering on Idiocy." *Capitalism Magazine.* Internet. April 25.

Malkin, Michelle. 2004. "The Illegal Immigration/Terrorist Connection, Part XXXLVIII." Internet. October 22.

Moore, Art. 2002. "Illegal Immigration Fueling Aims of Hispanic Radicals." WorldNetDaily.com.

Poston, Dudley L., Jr., Steven A Camarota, and Amanda K. Baumle. 2003. "Remaking the Political Landscape: The Impact of Illegal and Legal Immigration on Congressional Apportionment." Panel Discussion. October.

Tienda, Marta. 2002. "Demography and the Social Contract." Demography. November, 587–616.

ONE FINAL WORD

America as we know her will cease to exist unless Americans stop the current trends.

America is in peril. Various forces seek to destroy what her Founding Fathers established by the grace of God.

The United States of America was founded as a Christian nation, for that is what the vast majority of Americans were. I believe the majority of Americans still are Christians. A nation is what its people are.

America was intended to be a Holy Land, divinely set apart by God as a light shining on a hill. Right now, America is in shackles and her freedom is in jeopardy. A people may never secure its freedom once and for all time; it must be ready to forever pay the price to preserve its freedom until the Almighty restores the lost paradise.

Americans obviously have tough decisions to make.

PROPHETIC WARNINGS
TO AMERICA

"If men, through fear, fraud, or mistake, should in terms renounce or give up any natural right, the eternal law of reason and the grand end of society would absolutely vacate such renunciation. The right to freedom being the gift of god, it is not in the power of man to alienate this gift and voluntarily become a slave."

—Samuel Adams
The Father of the American Revolution

"We do not have a government armed with suffered power to tame the animal passions of mankind. The Constitution is made only for a moral and a religious people. It is wholly inadequate for the government of any other."

—President John Adams

"If ever time should come, when vain and aspiring men shall possess the highest seats in Government, our country will stand in need of its experienced patriots to prevent its ruin."

—Samuel Adams

"Among the natural rights of the Colonists are these: First, a right to life; Secondly, to liberty; Thirdly, to property; together with the right to support and defend them in the best manner they can."

—Samuel Adams
"Rights of the Colonists," November 1772

"You need only reflect that one of the best ways to get yourself a reputation as a dangerous citizen these days is to go about repeating the very phrases which our founding fathers used in their struggle for independence."

—C. A. Beard

"When they came to Capernaum those who collected tax money came to Peter and said, 'Does your master not pay taxes?' He said, 'Yes.' When he came into the house Jesus stopped him, saying, 'What do you think, Simon? From whom do the kings of the earth take custom or taxes? From their own children, or from strangers?' Peter replied, 'From strangers.' Jesus said, 'Then the children are free' " (*Mt. 17:24–26*).

—The Holy Bible

"Property: Rightful dominion over external objects; ownership; the unrestricted and exclusive right to a thing; Property is the highest right a man can have to anything."

—Black's Law Dictionary, Second Edition, 1891

"Income Tax: A tax on the yearly profits arising from property, professions, trades, and offices."

—Black's Law Dictionary Second Edition, 1891

"Our task of creating a Socialist America can only succeed when those who would resist us have been totally disarmed."

—Sarah Brady

"I do solemnly swear that I will support and defend the Constitution of the United States against all enemies, foreign and domestic; that I will bear true faith and allegiance to the same; that I take this obligation freely, without any mental reservation or purpose of evasion: and that I will well and faithfully discharge the duties of the office on which I am about to enter. So help me, God."

—Congressional Oath of Office

"As civil rulers, not having their duty to the people duly before them, may attempt to tyrannize, and as the military forces which must be occasionally raised to defend our country, might pervert their power to the injury of their fellow citizens, the people are confirmed by the next article [the Second Amendment] in their right to keep and bear their private arms."

*—Trence Coxe under the pseudonym "A Pennsylvanian"
From "Remarks on the First Part of the Amendments to
the Federal Constitution," Published in the Philadelphia
Federal Gazette,
18 June 1789*

"Find out just what the people will submit to, and you have found out the exact amount of injustice and wrong which will be imposed upon them; and these will continue until they are resisted with either words or blows, or with both. The limits of tyrants are prescribed by the endurance of those whom they oppress."

—Frederick Douglas (1857)

"The hardest thing in the world to understand is the income tax."

—Albert Einstein

"It is well that the people of the nation do not understand our banking and monetary system, for if they did, I believe there would be a revolution before tomorrow morning"

—Henry Ford

"Those who give up essential liberties for temporary safety deserve neither liberty nor safety."
—Benjamin Franklin

"Step by Step the International Financiers and those who represent them gain ownership of real assets as collateral for the debt interest. Now these assets are not directly acquired by the Federal Reserve but the wealth is acquired through the continual process of inflation which is merely the result of the flooding of the economy with fiat money. This system ensures that the wealth is slowly transferred from the middle class to the upper class."
—Fraser and Beeston

"What, sir, is the use of a militia? It is to prevent the establishment of a standing army, the bane of liberty... Whenever Governments mean to invade the rights and liberties of the people, they always attempt to destroy the militia, in order to raise an army upon their ruins."
—Representative Elbridge Gerry, Massachusetts,
I Annals of Congress at 750, 8/17/1789

"The legal right of the taxpayer to decrease the amount of what otherwise would be his taxes or altogether avoid them by means which the law permits, cannot be doubted."
—Gregory v. Helvering, 293 U.S. 465

"The great object is that everyman be armed. Everyone who is able may have a gun."
—Patrick Henry
At the Virginia Convention on the ratification of the Constitution

"I know not what course others may take, but as for me, give me liberty or give me death."

—*Patrick Henry*

"The best yardstick of the effectiveness of the fight against Communism is the fury of the smear attacks against the fighter."

—*J. Edgar Hoover*

"The democracy will cease to exist when you take away from those who are willing to work and give to those who would not."

—*President Thomas Jefferson*

"To compel a man to subsidize with his taxes the propagation of ideas which he disbelieves and abhors is sinful and tyrannical."

—*President Thomas Jefferson*

"When we get piled upon one another in large cities, as in Europe, we shall become as corrupt as Europe."

—*President Thomas Jefferson*

"Still one thing more, fellow citizens, a wise and frugal government which shall restrain men from injuring one another, shall leave them otherwise free to regulate their own pursuits of industry and improvement, and shall not take from the mouth of labor the bread it has earned. This is the sum of good government."

—*President Thomas Jefferson, First Inaugural Address*

"I predict future happiness for Americans if they can prevent the government from wasting the labors of the people under the pretense of taking care of them."

—*President Thomas Jefferson*

"Fear can only prevail when victims are ignorant of the facts."
—President Thomas Jefferson

"The strongest reason for the people to retain the right to keep and bear arms is, as a last resort, to protect themselves against tyranny in government."
—President Thomas Jefferson

"No free man shall ever be debarred the use of arms."
—President Thomas Jefferson

"Peace, commerce, and honest friendship with all nations, entangling alliances with none."
—President Thomas Jefferson, First Inaugural Address

"A government that is large enough to supply everything you need is large enough to take everything you have."
—President Thomas Jefferson

"I sincerely believe that banking institutions are more dangerous to our liberties than standing armies. If the American people ever allow private banks to control the issue of their currency, first by inflation, then by deflation, the banks and corporations that will grow up around the banks will deprive the people of all property until their children wake up homeless on the continent their fathers conquered."
—President Thomas Jefferson

"The tree of liberty must be watered periodically with the blood of tyrants and patriots alike. It is its natural manure."
—President Thomas Jefferson

"A strong body makes the mind strong. As to the species of exercises, I advise the gun. While this gives moderate exercise to the body, it gives boldness, enterprise and independence to the mind. Games played with the ball and others of that nature, are too violent for the body and stamp no character on the mind. Let your gun therefore be the constant companion of your walks."
—President Thomas Jefferson

"The high office of President has been used to foment a plot to destroy the American's freedom, and before I leave office I must inform the citizen of his plight."
—President John F. Kennedy
At Columbia University, ten days before his assassination

"We shall cause the United States to spend itself to destruction."
—Lenin

"This nation can never be conquered from without. If it is ever to fall it will be from within."
—President Abraham Lincoln

"As usurpation is the exercise of power, which another hath a right to; so tyranny is the exercise of power beyond right, which nobody can have a right to."
—John Locke, "Of Civil Government," 1689

"I believe there are more instances of the abridgment of freedom of the people by gradual and silent encroachment of those in power than by violent and sudden usurpations."
—President James Madison

"The Federal Reserve Bank is 'a super-state' controlled by international bankers and international industrialists

acting together to enslave the world for their own pleasure."
—Former Congressman Louis McFadden
Former Chairman, House Committee on Banking and Currency

"We have in this country one of the most corrupt institutions the world has ever known. I refer to the Federal Reserve Board and the Federal Reserve Banks...They are, not government institutions. They are private monopolies which prey upon the people of these United States for the benefit of themselves and their foreign customers..."
—Senator Louis T. McFadden
Chairman of the U.S. Banking & Currency Commission

"Those that create and issue the money and credit direct the policies of government and hold in their hands the destiny of the people."
—Reginald McKenna
Former President of the Midlands Bank of England

"In the United States today we have in effect two governments. We have the duly constituted government. Then we have an independent, uncontrolled and uncoordinated government in the Federal Reserve System, operating the money powers reserved to Congress by the Constitution"
—Congressman Wright Patman
Former Chairman of the House Banking Committee

"Patriotism means to stand by the country. It does not mean to stand by the President or any other public office save exactly to the degree in which he himself stands by the country."
—President Theodore Roosevelt

"No one is bound to obey an unconstitutional law and no courts are bound to enforce it."
—*Sixteenth American Jurisprudence*
Second Edition, Section 177

"The highest level of prosperity occurs when there is a free-market economy and a minimum of government regulations."
—*Adam Smith, "The Wealth of Nations"*
"'Income,' as used in the statute should be given the meaning so as not to include everything that comes in. The true function of the words 'gain' and 'profit' is to limit the meaning of the word income."
—*So. Pacific v. Lower, 238 F 847*

"All socialism involves slavery."
—*Herbert Spencer*

"All government without the consent of the governed is the very definition of slavery."
—*Jonathan Swift*

"The tax power has been used by the national government as a weapon to take over, one by one, subjects traditionally within the orbit of state police power."
—*Chief Justice Taft*

"All laws which are repugnant to the Constitution are null and void."
—*U.S. Supreme Court*
Marbury v. Madison, 2 Cranch 5 U.S. (1803)

"None are more hopelessly enslaved than those who falsely believe they are free."
—*Johann W. Von Goethe*

"It is impossible to rightly govern the world without God or the Bible." And "Reason and experience forbid us to expect public morality in the absence of religious principle."

—*President George Washington*

"Government is not reason; it is not eloquence; it is force! Like fire, it is a dangerous servant and a fearful master."

—*President George Washington*

"God grants liberty only to those who love it, and are always ready to guard and defend it."

—*Daniel Webster*

"An Unconstitutional Act is not a law; it confers no rights; it imposes no duties; it affords no protection; it creates no office; it is, in legal contemplation, as inoperative as though it had never been passed."

—*U.S. Supreme Court Norton V. Shelby County, 118 U.S. 425, 442*

"If we abide by the principles taught in the Bible, our nation will go on prospering."

—*Daniel Webster*

"God grants liberty only to those who love it, and are always ready to guard and defend it."

—*Daniel Webster*

"One of the main purposes for the control and power of the Establishment media is to keep the masses deceived and ignorant about their rights and oppressions of their rights."

—*Charles Weisman*

COMMUNIST RULES
FOR REVOLUTION

Captured by the Allies in Dusseldorf, Germany
1919

A. Corrupt the young, get them away from religion. Get them interested in sex. Make them superficial, destroy their ruggedness.

B. Get control of all means of publicity and thereby:
1. Get people's mind off their government by focusing their attention on athletics, sexy books, and plays and other trivialities.
2. Divide the people into hostile groups by constantly harping on controversial matters of no importance.
3. Destroy the people's faith in their natural leaders by holding the latter up to contempt, ridicule, and obloquy.
4. Always preach true democracy but seize power as fast and as ruthlessly as possible.
5. By encouraging government extravagance, destroy its credit, produce fear of inflation with rising prices and general discontent.
6. Foment unnecessary strikes in vital industries, encourage civil disorders, and foster a lenient and soft attitude on the part of government toward such disorders.
7. By specious argument cause the breakdown of the old moral virtues: honesty, sobriety, continence, faith in the pledged word, ruggedness.

C. Cause the registration of all firearms on some pretext, with a view of confiscating them and leaving the population helpless.

THE COMMUNIST TAKEOVER OF AMERICA

45 Declared Goals

Communist Goals (1963) Congressional Record-- Appendix, pp. A34-A35 January 10, 1963

Current Communist Goals EXTENSION OF REMARKS OF HON. A. S. HERLONG, JR. OF FLORIDA IN THE HOUSE OF REPRESENTATIVES Thursday, January 10, 1963 .

Mr. HERLONG. Mr. Speaker, Mrs. Patricia Nordman of De Land, Fla., is an ardent and articulate opponent of communism, and until recently published the *De Land Courier*, which she dedicated to the purpose of alerting the public to the dangers of communism in America.

At Mrs. Nordman's request, I include in the RECORD, under unanimous consent, the following "Current Communist Goals," which she identifies as an excerpt from "The Naked Communist," by Cleon Skousen:

[From "The Naked Communist," by Cleon Skousen]

1. U.S. acceptance of coexistence as the only alternative to atomic war.
2. U.S. willingness to capitulate in preference to engaging in atomic war.

3. Develop the illusion that total disarmament [by] the United States would be a demonstration of moral strength.
4. Permit free trade between all nations regardless of Communist affiliation and regardless of whether or not items could be used for war.
5. Extension of long-term loans to Russia and Soviet satellites.
6. Provide American aid to all nations regardless of Communist domination.
7. Grant recognition of Red China. Admission of Red China to the U.N.
8. Set up East and West Germany as separate states in spite of Khrushchev's promise in 1955 to settle the German question by free elections under supervision of the U.N.
9. Prolong the conferences to ban atomic tests because the United States has agreed to suspend tests as long as negotiations are in progress.
10. Allow all Soviet satellites individual representation in the U.N.
11. Promote the U.N. as the only hope for mankind. If its charter is rewritten, demand that it be set up as a one-world government with its own independent armed forces. (Some Communist leaders believe the world can be taken over as easily by the U.N. as by Moscow. Sometimes these two centers compete with each other as they are now doing in the Congo.)
12. Resist any attempt to outlaw the Communist Party.
13. Do away with all loyalty oaths.
14. Continue giving Russia access to the U.S. Patent Office.
15. Capture one or both of the political parties in the United States.
16. Use technical decisions of the courts to weaken

basic American institutions by claiming their activities violate civil rights.

17. Get control of the schools. Use them as transmission belts for socialism and current Communist propaganda. Soften the curriculum. Get control of teachers' associations. Put the party line in textbooks.

18. Gain control of all student newspapers.

19. Use student riots to foment public protests against programs or organizations which are under Communist attack.

20. Infiltrate the press. Get control of book-review assignments, editorial writing, policy-making positions.

21. Gain control of key positions in radio, TV, and motion pictures.

22. Continue discrediting American culture by degrading all forms of artistic expression. An American Communist cell was told to "eliminate all good sculpture from parks and buildings, substitute shapeless, awkward and meaningless forms."

23. Control art critics and directors of art museums. "Our plan is to promote ugliness, repulsive, meaningless art."

24. Eliminate all laws governing obscenity by calling them "censorship" and a violation of free speech and free press.

25. Break down cultural standards of morality by promoting pornography and obscenity in books, magazines, motion pictures, radio, and TV.

26. Present homosexuality, degeneracy and promiscuity as "normal, natural, healthy."

27. Infiltrate the churches and replace revealed religion with "social" religion. Discredit the Bible and emphasize the need for intellectual maturity, which does not need a "religious crutch."

28. Eliminate prayer or any phase of religious expression in the schools on the ground that it violates the principle of "separation of church and state."
29. Discredit the American Constitution by calling it inadequate, old-fashioned, out of step with modern needs, a hindrance to cooperation between nations on a worldwide basis.
30. Discredit the American Founding Fathers. Present them as selfish aristocrats who had no concern for the "common man."
31. Belittle all forms of American culture and discourage the teaching of American history on the ground that it was only a minor part of the "big picture." Give more emphasis to Russian history since the Communists took over.
32. Support any socialist movement to give centralized control over any part of the culture—education, social agencies, welfare programs, mental health clinics, etc.
33. Eliminate all laws or procedures which interfere with the operation of the Communist apparatus.
34. Eliminate the House Committee on Un-American Activities.
35. Discredit and eventually dismantle the FBI.
36. Infiltrate and gain control of more unions.
37. Infiltrate and gain control of big business.
38. Transfer some of the powers of arrest from the police to social agencies. Treat all behavioral problems as psychiatric disorders which no one but psychiatrists can understand [or treat].
39. Dominate the psychiatric profession and use mental health laws as a means of gaining coercive control over those who oppose Communist goals.
40. Discredit the family as an institution. Encourage promiscuity and easy divorce.

41. Emphasize the need to raise children away from the negative influence of parents. Attribute prejudices, mental blocks and retarding of children to suppressive influence of parents.
42. Create the impression that violence and insurrection are legitimate aspects of the American tradition; that students and special-interest groups should rise up and use ["]united force ["] to solve economic, political or social problems.
43. Overthrow all colonial governments before native populations are ready for self-government.
44. Internationalize the Panama Canal.
45. Repeal the Connally reservation so the United States cannot prevent the World Court from seizing jurisdiction [over domestic problems. Give the World Court jurisdiction] over nations and individuals alike.

Sources are listed below.

Microfilm: California State University at San Jose Clark Library, Government Floor Phone (408) 924-2770 Microfilm Call Number: J 11.R5

Congressional Record, Vol. 109 88th Congress, 1st Session Appendix Pages A1–A2842 Jan. 9-May 7, 1963 Reel 12

KING SOLOMON
REFUTES COMMUNISM

"My son, if sinners entice thee, consent thou not. If they say, Come with us, let us lay wait for blood, let us lurk privily for the innocent without cause: Let us swallow them up alive as the grave; and whole, as those that go down into the pit: We shall find all precious substance, we shall fill our houses with spoil: Cast in thy lot among us; let us all have one purse: My son, walk not thou in the way with them; refrain thy foot from their path: For their feet run to evil, and make haste to shed blood. Surely in vain the net is spread in the sight of any bird. And they lay wait for their *own* blood; they lurk privily for their *own* lives. So *are* the ways of every one that is greedy of gain; *which* taketh away the life of the owners thereof."

—*King Solomon*
Proverbs 1:10-19, KJV

ABOUT THE AUTHOR

CHAPLAIN (MAJOR) JAMES F. LINZEY, ARNG (RET.) is a retired United States Army Chaplain, having served a combined total of nearly twenty-four years of active duty and reserve duty. Jim began his military career in the United States Air Force on November 5, 1985. On January 4, 1998, he left the Air Force to join the Army. Among Jim's assignments were tours of duty at Maxwell Air Force Base, Montgomery, Alabama, where he attended Air University. Among many subjects, he focused his studies on Leadership Awareness, Team Awareness and Team Leadership. Among the Professional Military Education schools and courses he attended were the Air Force Officers' Orientation Course, the Chaplains Officers' Basic Course, the Chaplains Officers' Advanced Course, the Squadron Officers' School, the Combined Arms and Services Staff School, and the Command and General Staff College.

Military assignments over his twenty-four-year career include Command Chaplain, 5035th Garrison Support Unit, Fort Bliss, Texas; Command Chaplain, Cluster III, Operation Noble Eagle II, White Sands Missile Range, New Mexico, under the Department of Homeland

Security; and Chaplain for the Officer Candidate School at Fort Mead, South Dakota. In the course of his career, Jim trained military personnel in principles and practices of character-based leadership in Joint-Military Leadership Training at the Armed Forces Staff College and aboard the USS *Briscoe* at the Naval Air Station, Norfolk, Virginia, and in the Quartermaster's Officers' Basic Course and Non-commissioned Officers seminars at Fort Lee, Virginia. Jim applied his training while serving on the Leadership Panel at the United States Army Cadet Command's Leader's Training Course at Fort Knox, Kentucky, as its first full-time chaplain. Jim retired from the U.S. Army on June 29, 2009 with an Honorable Discharge at the rank of Major.

Jim attended the Billy Graham School of Evangelism in Ashville, North Carolina. He received a Bachelor of Arts degree from Vanguard University of Southern California, Costa Mesa, California; a Master of Divinity degree from Fuller Theological Seminary, Pasadena, California; and a Doctor of Divinity degree from Kingsway Theological Seminary, Des Moines, Iowa.

Other appearances, including media consist of ABC News, CBS News, CNN News, the Christian Broadcasting Network and the *Glenn Beck Show*. He was a guest on Daystar Television Network, God's Learning Channel, SON Broadcasting Network and Trinity Broadcasting Network. Jim hosted his own television series, which aired on various networks around the world. He also served as a missionary and conducted evangelistic crusades. He supports missions projects in Mexico, the Philippines, India and Africa.

Jim is listed in *Who's Who in America, Who's Who in the World,* the *International Centre of Biography in Cambridge, England,* and *2000 Intellectuals of the 21st Century.*

78

www.ingramcontent.com/pod-product-compliance
Lightning Source LLC
Chambersburg PA
CBHW070914280326
41934CB00008B/1723